Dedicated Dogs

David R Morgan

Illustrated by Anastasia Kotelnikova

Dedicated Dogs

This is a work of fiction.

Text and Illustrations copyrighted

by David Morgan ©2021

Library of Congress Control Number: 2020912465

All rights reserved. No part of this book may be

reproduced, transmitted, or stored in an information retrieval

system in any form or by any means,

graphic, electronic, or mechanical without prior written

permission from the author.

Printed in the United States of America

A 2 Z Press LLC

PO Box 582

Deleon Springs, FL 32130

bestlittleonlinebookstore.com

sizemore3630@aol.com

440-241-3126

ISBN: 978-1-946908-42-1

Dedication

**To Bex and Toby,
Who are 'paw'-fect!**

Welcome to this little book about dogs!
There are so many awesome varieties,

That are all truly loved by everyone, you see.

Dogs came from a large group called Canidae (Kan ih dee),
That includes the dog, the wolf, the fox, and the coyote.

But *each* is the 'very best dog' of all!

There is a dog to suit every human need,
They are fun-enhancing and very useful indeed!

Did you know there are 600 million dogs on the Earth?
And that each of the 159 breeds has its very own special worth.

There are terriers and working and
non – working dogs, hounds, and labradors,
herding dogs, toys, sporting breeds and more.

Border collies, pugs, poodles and Alsatians,
Pekineses, Great Danes, Shi tzus, and the dalmatian!

Some dogs gladly herd all your hilarious sheep,

Dogs love fetching sticks and bringing them back,
But their owners are the leaders of their little pack.

It's good to hear your doggy's distinct bark,
When you sneak in from being out late before dark.

A Russian dog named Laika,
was the first animal in space,
And in 1957, there were stamps
made showing this little dog's face.

David's dog Rusty never needs to talk,
He always knows when Rusty wants a walk.

When the garbage is strewn and the toys tossed about,
"Ok! Ok!" David understands it is time to go out!

She wags her tail and barks,
It's time to play,
Millie's puppy eyes always
get her, her way.

Princess and her Cavapoochon called Cosmo,
Are the cutest, magical pair wherever they go.

They shower 'happiness spells,' so no one is blue, Princess and Cosmo are a fairy tale come true.

And they can hear four times better than boys and girls as well!

Boys and girls have five million receptors in each of their noses, while our furry friends have 125 million of those to smell roses!

Did you know that dogs can vividly dream? They are much like boys and girls, so it seems.

Dogs see in color, not just black and white,
And their jaws are strong and can close very tight!

Crufts is a variety show with dogs on display,
Where each dog is special in its very own way.

A dog's sense of direction is really spot-on,
With great instinct to find where they're coming from.
And, no matter how long or how far you may roam,
A dog's wagging tail will welcome you home.

No one is more faithful that shows love so true,
Who tries to cheer you up when you're feeling blue.

A dog is so loyal it will stay with you till the end, That's why dogs are called man's very best friend!

The End

Dogs - Not only are they are man's best friend, they are women's best friends, children's best friends, and everyone's best friends! Some fun facts about dogs are:

1. The Labrador Retriever has been on the American Kennel Club's top 10 most popular breeds list for 25 consecutive years—longer than any other breed. And the Labrador Retriever is originally from Newfoundland.
2. Almost 1/2 of all dogs in the United States sleep in their owner's bed.
3. Over 1/2 of owners sign their dog's name on their holiday cards.
4. Rin Tin Tin, the famous German Shepherd, was nominated for an Academy Award.
5. The Australian Shepherd is not actually from Australia—they are an American breed.
6. Human blood pressure goes down when petting a dog. And so does the dog's.
7. There are over 75 million pet dogs in the U.S.—more than in any other country.
8. A recent study shows that dogs are among a small group of animals who show voluntary unselfish kindness towards others without any reward. This is one fact dog lovers have known all along.

David R Morgan lives in England. He is a talented full-time teacher and writer.

He has written music journalism, poetry and children's books. His books for children include : 'The Strange Case of William Whipper-Snapper', three 'Info Rider' books for Collins and 'Blooming Cats' which won the Acorn Award and was animated for television. He has also written a Horrible Histories biography : ' Spilling The Beans On Boudicca' and stories for Children's anthologies.

For the last 4 years he has been working on his Soundings Project with his son Toby, performing his own poetry/writing to Toby's original music. This work is on YouTube, Spotify and Soundcloud.

Other Books by David R. Morgan

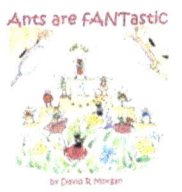 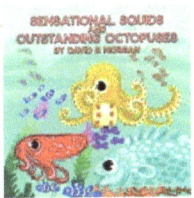   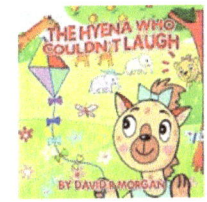

  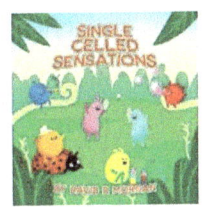  

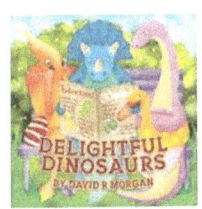 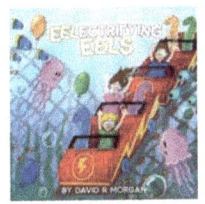   

And many more to come!

A2Z Press LLC

A2Z Press LLC published this work. A2Z Press LLC is a publishing company created by Terrie Sizemore for the purpose of publishing literary works by new and aspiring writers. All content is G-rated. We welcome your submissions of ideas for children's literature as well as adult and self-help topics. Science and medicine, holidays and other interesting topics are all welcome. Submit queries to sizemore3630@aol.com or PO Box 582 Deleon Springs, FL 32130

Visit our Website

Visit terriesizemorestoryteller.com or bestlittleonlinebookstore.com for our latest titles and gifts for everyone.

www.ingramcontent.com/pod-product-compliance
Lightning Source LLC
Chambersburg PA
CBHW051400110526
44592CB00023B/2900